ONE WEEK FRENCH MASTERY

The Complete Beginner's Guide to Learning French in just 1 Week!

Detailed Step by Step Process to Understand the Basics

By Erica Stewart and Chantal Abadie

DISCLAIMER

The information provided herein is stated to be truthful and consistent, in that any liability, in terms of inattention or otherwise, by any usage or abusage of any policies, processes, or directions contained within is the solitary and utter responsibility of the recipient reader. Under no circumstances will any legal responsibility or blame be held against the publisher for any reparation, damages, or monetary loss due to the information herein, either directly or indirectly. Respective authors hold all rights not held by publisher.

Note from the Author:

Learning a new language is such a challenge, but enriching on so many levels. It's not only an intellectual challenge, but imagine transforming your travel experiences, allowing you to connect with new and interesting people, or even live or study overseas. In essence, it's a journey to become more open minded about the world, discovering amazing new people in the process.

As an educator for more than 20 years, I'm a fan of teaching others. And there is no greater challenge than to learn a language. However, learning is not the obsessive command of structures and vocabulary, but the willingness to overcome our most basic fears and insecurities. Over the course of this book, I will convey enough knowledge of French so that you will be able to read, listen, and interact with people in this new language with the knowledge that will inspire confidence. From here, practice will take you to a new level of accomplishments and a lifetime of enjoyment!

In learning French, you will be facing 5 basic but important challenges; grammar, vocabulary, slang and colloquialism, pronunciation and variations of the language. In this book, I will lay out the fundamentals of each of these stepping stones in an easy to understand method.

I want to especially thank Chantal Abadie for her guidance and instruction in helping me put together this material. It's been such a privilege to have her as my French teacher and I've learned so much about this fascinating culture and the wonderful history of France. Reading original masterpieces by Balzac, Flaubert, Voltaire and Dumas and traveling to Paris, Nice, Marseille or Lyon with the ability to interact with the locals in their own language has been a transformative experience! I invite you to read on and begin a fascinating learning experience.

Best,

Erica Stewart

Chapter Index

Introduction

This book contains the secrets to mastering the French language, along with easy-to-follow guidelines and lesson plans designed to get you on the road toward French fluency.

How great would it be to access the world of over one million native French speakers by sharing their beautiful language with them? In the United States, French is one of the most studied languages second to English. As a national standard in most American high schools, you've probably taken a two-year French language course. But how much vocabulary have you actually retained from the course after graduation? Chances are your French skills never actually came to life outside of the classroom.

You've most likely never reached a level where you can actually communicate in French due to the elongated, slow pace of traditional language courses. Linguistic experts generally agree that intensity trumps length of study. This means that you learn more when you dive into a new language at full force rather than prolonging the learning process over the course of several months—in some cases, years. In line with this notion, this book divides the French language into bite-sized portions designed for fast-paced learning. Believe it or not, crammed knowledge provided through crash courses promotes better retention.

Learning a new language calls for equal parts determination and commitment. But just because a language is new to you doesn't mean it's entirely foreign. French is actually considered one of the easiest languages for native English speakers to adopt. Both languages are derived from Latin roots, thus giving them many similarities. In fact, if you're a fluent English speaker, you are already equipped with tons of French vocabulary. That's the magic of romance languages. English and French share hundreds of words that have similar meanings and sounds—also known as cognates. French words like *seconde* and *calendrier* are translated to the English words "second" and "calendar," respectively. Notice that the French cognates for these two English words remain nearly unchanged. To make matters easier, French grammar and sentence structure are of a simpler nature than English.

Learning French is great for travel, for living abroad, or for the sole purpose of brain training. It creates a bond and sets you apart as an American. It's almost like having a second soul. Whether your goal is to become a bilingual speaker or a polyglot, having a thorough knowledge of French opens doors to better work opportunities as well as other Romance languages like

Spanish and Italian. Let this book serve as a guide for ultimately mastering the French language. The key is to delve deeply into the language and aim for a brain melt. It's the best way to retain lasting knowledge and reach a level of communication with native French speakers. After all, the best treasure is uncovered when you dig deep.

Chapter 1: Secrets to Learning French in Record Time

The Romance language of French belongs to the Indo-European family. It is the second most widespread language, owing to France's overseas expansion over a span of several hundred years. French is the official language of 29 countries including France, Canada, Belgium, and Monaco. Currently, there are nearly 300 million French speakers worldwide, with a third of those being native speakers. This number is expected to rise by at least 50% by the year 2050. Considering the ease by which French can be picked up, this doubled increase of speakers seems feasible.

Before you begin the transition from monolingual to bilingual, it's advisable to arm yourself with tips and tricks to simplify the learning process. This chapter lists ten hacks that will enable you to get in the right mind frame for learning French while also speeding up your progress.

1.) Do it with Passion or Not at All

Passion is the driving force behind perfection—or in your case, fluency. Joseph Campbell once said, "Passion will move men beyond themselves, beyond their shortcomings and failures." As mentioned earlier, two important ingredients for learning a new language is dedication and determination. These two things are both derived from passion. You've got to *want* to learn

French and be excited about it as well. Otherwise, your motivation level will drop halfway through. Bottom line: be passionate to succeed, and do whatever it takes to reach your language goals.

2.) Stick with Your Language-Learning Strategy

Before diving into the deep end of the French language pool, it's important to lay out a realistic learning plan. Fortunately for you, this book serves as a guideline for your language-learning strategy. While the strategies here may not work for everyone, it's a relatively easy guideline to follow. Adopt the learning methods that work for you, and discard those that don't. There is no single approach that works for all, but this book outlines a universal language-learning strategy that is backed by linguistic experts.

3.) Memorize the High Frequency French Words

This language-learning hack is easily the most crucial. It's a step you wouldn't want to skip. Learning a total of three-hundred basic words is the best place to start—and it goes for all foreign languages. Experts generally agree that a thorough knowledge of 300 to 500 most frequently used words of a language forms a great baseline. This is because only a few hundred words make up 65% of all written and verbal material. In Chapter 5, we will go over the list of high frequency

French words.

4.) Focus on Relevant Content

One of the most counterproductive things you could do when attempting to learn a new language is accumulate knowledge of irrelevant material. Knowledge *is* power, but in the case of learning a new language, irrelevant knowledge leaves you powerless. Identify your reasons for wanting to take up French, as well as your interests. If you have a penchant for French cuisine, photography, or fashion, prioritize the words and key phrases associated with those particular interests. Vocabulary outside of those interests should be a second priority. If you plan to visit France, focus first on relevant vocabulary associated with travel. You get the idea.

5.) Recognize True Word Friends

Cognates give you a huge head start in the French language. Most Romance languages share hundreds of similar words with identical definitions and comparable spellings. Due to this special little quirk, you're not actually starting French from scratch. Dozens of English words ending in *-tion* such as "action" and "communication" are spelled the same in French—the only difference being pronunciation and altered stress. This is why Romance languages are the most commonly studied second languages in the United States as many words from those languages are borrowed from English. Chapter 4 lists many French English cognates for you to study in order to jump-start your progress and improve your French.

6.) Interact in French

Strengthening your French skills means immersing yourself in the language. Intensify your learning strategy by regularly engaging in French conversation and dabbling in French culture, e.g. movies and books. One great learning method used by countless beginners is interacting with a language buddy live online. Interpals.net and mylanguageexchange.com are two huge online language communities where users exchange languages with live native speakers of their target language. There, you can find French speakers eager to learn the English language from you. It's a give-and-take process that allows users to borrow words and phrases from each other.

7.) Take Advantage of Free Language Tools

After all, the best things in life are free. There are countless resources out there which aim to teach you the basics of your target language and provide audio to help with your pronunciation. Since this book is simply a written guide, I highly recommend using online verbal resources for the first few days to get yourself accustomed to French. Feel free as well to use audio resources as a supplement to this guidebook.

Free apps like DuoLingo and Memrise offer great French courses that utilize images and audio dialogues for optimal learning. Forvo.com is a helpful pronunciation dictionary that you can use as a supplemental resource for this book. Rhinospike.com is another huge online database that allows you to hear words and expressions spoken aloud by native French speakers.

8.) Practice Intensely

Your progress should be measured in devoted hours instead of years. Believe it or not, there is a language-learning shortcut you can take. Most experts agree that practicing a new language every day for at least three devoted hours is the key to quick fluency. Prolonged practice that spans years is the wrong way; shortened practice spanning six months is the right way. Fluency in a new language is possible in less than a year with intense practice. Even after the three hours of allotted practice time, it's recommended to continue practicing throughout the day by speaking French aloud or by simply listening to French audio in the form of music and movies. Intense study pays off in the short-term.

It's important to disregard the notion that there's only so much information your brain can process at any given time. Brain overload is a myth. Your learning capacity is virtually limitless. Learning between 50 to 100 new French words every day along with 25 phrases is the way to go.

9.) Repetition Generates Retention

R. Collier once said, "Success is the sum of all small efforts repeated day in and day out." Learning a new language is based on repetition. You've got to hammer a word or phrase into your head over and over again until you remember it. Repetition is the mother of all learning. Avoid putting long gaps between study sessions, as doing so will ensure you retain valuable information.

10.) Carry a Dictionary

A dictionary is the most valuable resource available in the world of language learning. Carry a French-English dictionary with you everywhere you go right from the start. Whether it's a phone app or a physical pocket dictionary, the key is to be able to consult it at a moment's notice. A dictionary is great for reference during interactions with native French speakers without disrupting the flow of conversation. You could even use it in line with upholding rule #8 above. At idle moments throughout the day—while waiting in line or being stuck in traffic—simply whip out your French-English dictionary and look through it. This way, you're not wasting any valuable opportunities for study and practice. You could even learn an extra dozen new French words each time by simply carrying a dictionary while you're on the go.

Chapter 2: French Alphabet and Accent Marks

The French language consists of all 26 letters of the English alphabet, plus a few add-ons. The table below lists the letters of the French alphabet accompanied by their suggested French pronunciation.

English Letter	**French Pronunciation**
A	*ahh*
B	*bay*
C	*say*
D	*day*
E	*euh*
F	*eff*
G	*zhay*
H	*ahsh*
I	*ee*

J	*zhee*
K	*kah*
L	*el*
M	*em*
N	*en*
O	*oh*
P	*pay*
Q	*koo*
R	*air*
S	*ess*
T	*tay*
U	*oo*
V	*vay*
W	*doo-bluh-vay*
X	*eex*
Y	*ee-grek*

Z	*zed*

There are eight additional letters used in the French language, bringing the total number of French letters to 34. When accent marks are used above or below certain letters, the pronunciation changes. For example, when the cedilla mark is used beneath the letter "C," it is pronounced /s/ rather than /k/.Since the letters below are frequently used in written French material, it's important to learn them all. Included are two ligatures commonly used in French.

French Letter	Pronunciation
Ç	*ss*
Œ	*oo*
Æ	*ay*
â	*ah*
ê	*eh*
î	*ih*
ô	*oah*

û	*oh*

Diacritic marks are frequently used alongside certain letters in French to signify pronunciation and meaning. Knowing the appropriate accent marks goes a long way in eliminating mistakes, and it's also essential for proper spelling. When accent marks are used, it changes the pronunciation and meaning of the word.

There are five distinct accent marks used in written French. Study the chart below to learn the role each accent mark plays in the French language.

Accent Mark	Purpose of Mark	Letters Used With Mark
aigu/acute (´)	Used to change the pronunciation of the letter "E" to *ay.*	e
grave (`)	Used to distinguish between homographs; e.g.	a, e, u

	ou vs *où*, meaning "or" and "where," respectively.	
circumflex (ˆ)	Used to indicate that the letter "S" used to follow the vowel; e.g. *forêt* (forest).	a, e, i, o, u
umlaut (¨)	Used when two vowels are next to each other, signifying that both must be pronounced; e.g. *naïve.*	e, i, u
cedilla (¸)	Used to change the pronunciation of the letter "C" from /k/ to /s/.	c

Chapter 3: French Pronunciation Guide

There's a captivating quality to spoken Romance languages that listeners find charming. Native French speakers have a way of melding words together that flows like honey. This way of speaking is exactly what you should strive to replicate.

French pronunciation, you might find, is a little intimidating due to silent letters and frequently used diacritics—not to mention, the many exemptions associated with pronunciation rules. This chapter aims to eliminate the confusion by breaking down French pronunciation in an easy-to-grasp manner. It's important to follow each rule below as they are laid out. Proper pronunciation is the difference between saying "You're fat" and "Thank you." Hence, it's crucial to pay close attention to detail and observe proper pronunciation in any language.

Stress

In comparison with English, French has a crisp sound that is more distinct. The intonation of French words has an even quality, but the last syllable is usually emphasized.

Pronouncing French Vowels

This is where it gets *really* confusing. You've already learned that vowels change in sound when attached to diacritics. Take the letter "E," for instance. The French language uses four distinct forms of the letter "E": e, é, è, and ê—and each form is pronounced differently from one another. To make matters more mind-boggling, the pronunciation of French vowels differ according to their placement in a word. The use of accent marks brings about another layer of confusion, but it's really not as complex as it seems. Below is a helpful guide for pronouncing French vowels:

Vowel	Pronunciation Rule	Example
A	Pronounced like the *a* in the English word "father."	*la* (the)
À	Also pronounced *ah*, and is used to distinguish between homographs.	*là* (there)
â	Also pronounced *ah*, but with a	*âne* (donkey)

	longer intonation.	
e (placed in the middle of a syllable)	Pronounced like the *ai* in the English word "hair."	*mer* (sea)
e (placed at the end of a syllable)	Pronounced like the *er* in the English word "her."	*le* (the)
e (placed at the end of a **word**)	This vowel is silent like the *e* in the English word "love."	*tasse* (cup)
é	Pronounced like the *ay* in the English word "may."	*été* (summer)
è	Pronounced like the *a* in the English word "care."	*père* (father)
ê	Also pronounced like the *a* in "care," and is used to	*tête* (head)

	distinguish between homographs.	
i, y	Pronounced like the *ee* in the English word "feet."	*ski* (skiing)
O	Pronounced like the *o* in the English word "hot."	*poste* (post office)
Ô	Pronounced like the *oa* in the English word "boat."	*hôtel* (hotel)
U	The best way to describe the sound "U" makes in French is to round your lips and say *ee*.	*vu* (seen)
oi	This vowel combination is	*foie* (liver)

	pronounced *wah.*	
ou	Pronounced like the *oo* in the English word "moon."	*roue* (wheel)
ai, ei	Pronounced like the *e* in the English word "beg."	*laine* (wool)
au, eau	These vowel combinations are both pronounced *oh.*	*au* (to the) *eau* (water)
eu, oeu	Both are pronounced like the *er* in the English word "her."	*neuf* (nine) *soeur* (sister)

For a quick a recap, remember the following rules:

- The vowels a, à, and â are all pronounced *ah,* except the latter is longer.

- The vowels è and ê are always pronounced *eh*. The same goes for e when placed in the middle of a syllable. When placed at the end of a word, however, e is silent.

Pronouncing French Consonants

Here's where French pronunciation gets easier. Consonants used in the French language has virtually the same sound as their English counterparts. Still, there are a few consonant rules to keep in mind. Refer to the table below—as well as the one above—as often as you like throughout the rest of this book.

Consonant	Pronunciation Rule	Example
c (placed before the letters E or I)	Pronounced like the *s* in the English word "sit."	*ceci* (this)
c (placed elsewhere)	Pronounced like the *c* in the English word "mic."	*car* (because)
Ç	Pronounced like the *ss* in the English word "miss."	ça (that)

ch	This consonant combination is pronounced like the *sh* in the English word "shun."	château (castle)
g (placed before the letters E or I)	Pronounced like the *s* in the English word "treasure."	général (general)
g (placed elsewhere)	Pronounced like the *g* in the English word "god."	gare (train station)
h	This consonant is silent like the *h* in the English word "hour."	hôtel (hotel)
j	Pronounced like the *s* in the English word "treasure."	je (I)
q, qu	Pronounced like the *k* in the English word	qui (who))

	"kin."	
R	This consonant is pronounced at the back of the throat, like the sound you make when you are gargling.	rire (laugh)
s (placed at the beginning of a word)	Pronounced like the *s* in the English word "sun."	salle (room)
s (placed between two vowels)	Pronounced like the *s* in the English word "rise."	rose (rose, pink)

Here's one more rule for consonants:

All consonants, with the exception of the letters C, F, L, and R, are usually silent when placed at the end of a word. For example, the French word "Paris" is pronounced *pair-ee*.

French Nasal Sounds

The French language is often described as having a unique nasally sound. These sounds are produced by preventing air from leaving the mouth, and released through the nose instead. In French, nasal sounds are voiced; in other words, the vocal cords vibrate to create the distinct sound.

Take, for instance, the three distinct nasal sounds in your native language of English: the *m* sound, *n* sound, and *ng* sound. Say the words "song" and "sing" aloud. Notice that the letter G is given little value, and that as you say the words, your tongue presses against your palate, blocking the air. The same concept goes for the nasal sounds in French. Study the table below to perfect your nasal pronunciations:

Nasal Sound	Pronunciation Rule	Example
om, on	Pronounced like the *ong* in the English word "song."	nom (name) non (no)
um, un	Pronounced like the *ung* in the English word "stung."	un (one brun (brown)
am, an	Both are	champ (field)

	pronounced *ahng.*	an (year)
em, en	Both are also pronounced *ahng.*	temps (time) en (in)
im, in	Both are pronounced like the *ang* in the English word "sang."	simple (easy vin (wine)
aim, ain, ein	All three are also pronounced like the *ang* in the English word "sang."	faim (hunger) bain (bath) plein (full)
ien	Pronounced *ee-ang* like the *ianc* in the name "Bianca."	bien (well)

French Variations of Syllables

Certain syllables of the French language are pronounced differently from English. The table below lists these particular variations.

Syllable	Pronunciation Rule	Example
er	When placed at the end of a word that consists of two or more syllables, it is pronounced *ay*.	parler (speak)
ez	When placed at the end of a word, it is pronounced *ay*.	nez (nose)
ail	When placed at the end of a word, it is pronounced *ah-ee*; the letter L is silent.	travail (work)
eil, eille	Pronounced *a-ee*; the letter L is silent.	soleil (sun) bouteille (bottle)
ill	Pronounced *ee-y*.	billet (ticket)
gn	Pronounced like the *ni* in the English word “onion.”	signal (signal)

Achieving the Distinct Flowing Sound

Some foreigners joke that native French speakers sound like they are speaking in cursive. With practice, you can connect your words and have them roll off your tongue in the same way in no time. Simply follow this rule to achieve a melodious effect:

If the first word of a phrase ends with a consonant, and the second word begins with either a vowel or a silent H, link the consonant to the beginning of the second word.

Confused? Let's break it down into simpler terms.

Take the French phrase *nous avons* into consideration Take a close look at this phrase and note that the first word ends with the consonant S while the second word begins with the vowel A:

nous avons

Connect the underlined letters. The term is pronounced *noo zah-vong.*

Here a few more pronunciation rules to remember:

Letter	Pronunciation	Example&

	Rule	Pronunciation
s, x	Pronounced like the *z* in the English word "zero."	deux ans (two years) *der-zahng*
d	Pronounced like the *t* in the English word "tiger."	un grand arbre (a large tree) *ung grahng-tahbr*
f	Pronounced like the *v* in the English word "vine."	neuf heures (nine o'clock) *ner-verr*

Chapter 4: True French-English Cognates

Now that you know how to properly pronounce French words, it's time to starting building your vocabulary.

You've already learned that French cognates have the same linguistic derivation as English. Learning cognates during the first couple of days is a great strategy and a good place to start as it provides you with a huge initial vocabulary. Cognates are super easy words to remember considering how alike they are in spelling and meaning with their English translations. This chapter focuses on French cognates of common English words. At the end of this lesson, you should be comfortable enough with French to move on to the nitty gritty of the language.

English	French
absolutely	absolument
abundance	abondance
accelerate	accélérer
accompany	accompagner

active	active
activity	activité
adventure	aventure
agent	agent
alarm	alarme
animal	animal
artist	artiste
banana	banane
battery	batterie
bicycle	bicyclette
blouse	blouse
cafeteria	cafétéria
camera	camér
captain	capitaine
celebrate	célébrer
color	couleur

confetti	confetti
curiosity	curiosité
decoration	décoration
delicate	délicat
delicious	délicieux-euse
dictionary	dictionnaire
doctor	docteur
dragon	dragon
electric	électrique
energy	énergie
enter	entrer
excuse	escuser
exotic	exotique
experience	expérience
extraordinary	extraordinaire
family	famille

famous	fameux-euse
fantastic	fantastique
festive	festive
flower	fleur
fruit	fruit
garden	jardin
generous	généreux
guide	guide
history	histoire
hotel	hôtel
hour	heure
imagine	imaginer
immigrant	immigrant
important	important
incredible	incrédible
information	information

instruction	instruction
justify	justifier
juvenile	juvénile
lemon	limon
list	liste
locate	localiser
magic	magique
manner	manière
manual	manuel
memory	mémoire
million	million
miniature	miniature
minutes	minutes
music	music
natural	naturel
necessity	nécessité

nervouse	nerveux
notice	notice
object	objet
occasion	occasion
ordinary	ordinaire
organize	organiser
palace	palais
paper	papier
park	parc
participate	participer
perfect	parfait
perfume	parfum
photograph	photographie
piano	piano
plant	plante
plate	plat

practice	pratique
problem	problème
radio	radio
rock	roche
route	route
secret	secret
simplify	simplifier
sofa	sofa
splendid	splendide
study	étudier
surprise	surprise
telephone	téléphone
television	télévision
terrible	terrible
tourist	touriste
traffic	trafic

uniform	uniforme
university	université
vegetables	végétales
verify	vérifier
version	version

Notice the similarities between the English words above and their French cognates. Some are even spelled exactly the same. Others are spelled the same, except the French cognates have accent marks, signifying a specific pronunciation. That's the beauty of learning a Romance language. With so many similarities between the two languages, it's virtually impossible to learn French from scratch.

Chapter 5: High Frequency French Words

Linguistics experts generally agree that a thorough knowledge of 3000-4000 words is all you need for complete fluency in any language. This notion isn't at all far-fetched considering your existing English skills. The entirety of the English language consists of over one million words, and only a small fraction of this total is still in current use. In fact, the most comprehensive English dictionaries only consist of approximately 150,000 word entries. Out of those 150,000 English words, you only need 2% for complete fluency in the English language.

The same goes for French. You only need a vocabulary of 3000 words to be considered fluent in French. This chapter, however, only lists the *core* vocabulary of French—which comes to a total of 300 easy words to remember. Since the 300 words listed in the table below makeup 65% of all written and verbal French material, it's recommended to memorize them all. Doing so practically ensures you have the capability to read, write, and speak a significant amount of French. Being able to communicate freely in French is the linguistic quality this book aims to provide.

The 300 high frequency French words is the perfect jumping-off point for beginners once you've learned common French cognates. In the end, the knowledge acquired from this chapter will make for an ideal baseline for more complex French vocabulary.

French Word	Part of Speech	English Translation
1. être	verb	to be; being
2. avoir	verb	to have
3. je	pronoun	I
4. de	preposition	of; by; with; from; than; in
5. ne	adverb; modifier	not
6. pas	1. adverb 2. noun	1. not 2. step; pace
7. le	1. article 2. pronoun	1. the; it 2. him

	(masculine)	
8. la	1. article 2. pronoun (feminine)	1. the; it 2. her
9. tu	pronoun	you
10. vous	pronoun	you; yourself
11. il	1. article 2. pronoun (masculine)	1. it 2. he
12. et	conjunction	and
13. à	preposition	in; to; with
14. un	article (used before a masculine singular noun)	a; an; one
15. l'	article (substitute for *la* and *le* before nouns beginning with a vowel)	the
16. qui	pronoun	1. who; whom

		2. that; which
17. aller	verb	to go
18. les	article (refers to a plural noun)	the; them
19. en	1. adverb 2. preposition	1. as 2. in; into; to
20. ça	pronoun	this; that
21. faire	verb	to do; make
22. tout	1. adjective 2. adverb	1. all; any; everything 2. very; quite
23. on	pronoun	we; you
24. que	pronoun	what; which; that
25. ce	pronoun	this; that
26. une	article (used before a feminine singular	a; an; one

	noun)	
27. mes	pronoun (used before a plural noun)	my
28. d’	preposition (used before words beginning with a vowel or silent H)	of; from; by; with; in; than
29. pour	preposition	for
30. se	pronoun	themselves; herself; himself
31. des	adjective (used before a plural noun)	some
32. dire	verb	to say; tell
33. pouvoir	verb	can; able to
34. vouloir	verb	to want
35. mais	conjunction	but
36. me	pronoun	me; myself

37. nous	pronoun	we; us
38. dans	preposition	in; into
39. elle	pronoun (feminine)	it; she
40. savoir	verb	to know
41. du	article	of the; from the
42. où	1. adverb 2. pronoun	1. where 2. that
43. y	1. pronoun 2. adverb	1. it 2. there
44. t’	pronoun (shortened form of *tu* and *te*; used before a vowel)	you; yourself
45. bien	1. adjective 2. adverb	1. well; good 2. very
46. voir	verb	to see
47. plus	adjective	more

48. non	adverb	no
49. te	pronoun	you; yourself
50. mon	pronoun (masculine)	my
51. au	article	to the; at the; in the
52. avec	preposition	with
53. moi	pronoun	me; I
54. si	1. adverb 2. conjunction 3. adjective	1. yes; so 2. if 3. such
55. quoi	pronoun (used interrogatively)	what
56. devoir	1. verb 2. noun	1. must; have to 2. duty; test
57. oui	adverb	yes
58. ils	pronoun (refers to a group of masculine	they

	nouns)	
59. comme	1. adverb 2. adjective	1. as; how 2. like; same
60. s’	pronoun (shortened form of *se*; used before a word a vowel or silent H)	themselves; herself; himself
61. venir	verb	occur; to come
62. sur	1. preposition 2. adjective	1. on; over; upon 2. sour
63. toi	pronoun	you
64. ici	adverb	here
65. rien	noun	nothing
66. lui	pronoun	it; he; him; her
67. bon	1. adjective	1. good; kind; right

	2. noun 3. adverb	2. voucher 3. then
68. là	adverb	then; here; there
69. suivre	verb	follow
70. pourquoi	adverb	why
71. parler	verb	speak; talk
72. prendre	verb	get; take
73. cette	demonstrative adjective	this; that
74. quand	conjunction	when; whenever
75. alors	adverb	so; then; hence
76. une chose	noun	thing; matter
77. par	preposition	through; per; by

78. son	possessive adjective	its; his; her
79. croire	verb	think; believe
80. aimer	verb	like; love
81. falloir	verb	must; have to
82. comment	1. adverb 2. pronoun	1. how 2. what
83. tres	adverb	very
84. ou	conjunction	or; either
85. passer	verb	cross; pass; go by
86. penser	verb	think
87. aussi	adverb	too; also; as well
88. jamais	adverb	never
89. attendre	verb	expect; wait for

90. trouver	verb	find
91. laisser	verb	leave
92. petit	1. adjective 2. noun	1. small; little; young 2. child
93. merci	common expression	Thank you.
94. même	1. adjective 2. adverb	1. same 2. as
95. sa	possessive adjective	its; her; his
96. ta	pronoun	your
97. autre	adjective	other; another; different
98. arriver	verb	arrive
99. ces	adjective	these; those
100. donner	verb	give; give away

101. regarder	verb	watch; look
102. encore	adverb	again; even; still
103. appeler	verb	call
104. est-ce que	adverb	is it
105. peu	adjective	few; not much
106. homme	noun	man
107. partir	verb	go; leave
108. ma	pronoun	my
109. toujours	adverb	always; still
110. jour	noun	day; daytime
111. femme	noun	woman; wife
112. temps	noun	time; weather
113. maintenant	adverb	now
114. notre	pronoun	our

115. vie	noun	life
116. deux	numerical adjective	two
117. mettre	verb	put on; wear
118. rester	verb	stay; remain
119. sans	preposition	without
120. seul	adjective	alone
121. arrêter	verb	stop
122. vraiment	adverb	truly; really
123. connaître	verb	experience; know
124. quelque	adjective	some; any
125. sûr	adjective	on; over
126. tuer	verb	kill
127. mourir	verb	die; pass away
128. demander	verb	ask
129. juste	adjective	fair; right;

		accurate
130. peut-être	adverb	maybe; perhaps
131. dieu	noun	God
132. fois	noun	time
133. oh	interjection	Oh!
134. père	noun	father
135. comprendre	verb	understand
136. sortir	verb	go out; take out
137. personne	1. noun 2. pronoun	1. person; individual 2. anyone; anybody
138. an	noun	year
139. trop	adverb	too much
140. chez	preposition	in; at; to

141. fille	noun	girl; daughter
142. aux	article	of the
143. monde	noun	world; people
144. ami	1. noun 2. adjective	1. friend 2. friendly
145. vrai	adjective	true; real; genuine
146. après	1. adverb 2. preposition	1. after; later 2. afterwards
147. mal	1. noun 2. adverb	1. trouble 2. wrongly; badly
148. besoin	noun	need; demand
149. accord	noun	agreement; harmony

150. ses	pronoun (plural)	its; her; his
151. avant	preposition	before
152. monsieur	noun	Mr.; gentleman
153. enfant	noun	infant; child
154. grand	1. adjective 2. noun	1. big; tall; great 2. big girl; big boy
155. entendre	verb	listen; hear; understand
156. voilà	preposition	there is; there are
157. chercher	verb	seek; look for
158. heure	noun	time; hour; age
159. mieux	1. adjective 2. noun	1. better; best

		2. improvemen t
160. tes	pronoun (plural)	your
161. aider	verb	help; aid
162. mère	noun	mother
163. déjà	adverb	already; before
164. beau	adjective	beautiful; pretty; lovely
165. essayer	verb	try; test
166. quel	pronoun (interrogative)	what; which
167. vos	pronoun (plural)	your
168. depuis	1. adverb 2. preposition	1. since 2. of; from
169. quelqu'un	pronoun	someone; somebody

170. beaucoup	adverb	a lot; many
171. revenir	verb	return; come back
172. donc	conjunction	so; therefore
173. plaire	verb	be successful
174. maison	noun	house; home
175. gens	noun	people
176. nuit	noun	night
177. ah	interjection	Ah!
178. soir	noun	evening
179. nom	noun	name
180. bonjour	greeting	hello
181. jouer	verb	play
182. leur	pronoun	their; theirs
183. finir	verb	finish; end
184. peur	noun	fear

185. mort	1. noun 2. adjective	1. death 2. dead
186. parce que	conjunction	for; because
187. perdre	verb	lose; miss
188. maman	noun	mom; mama
189. sentir	verb	smell; sniff
190. ouais	slang	yeah; yep
191. rentrer	verb	bring in; go in; come home
192. nos	pronoun	our
193. premier	1. adjective 2. noun	1. first; basic 2. first floor
194. problème	noun	problem
195. argent	noun	money; silver
196. quelle	pronoun	who; what;

	(interrogative)	which
197. vivre	verb	live; be alive; experience
198. rendre	verb	repay; return
199. dernier	1. noun 2. adjective	1. last 2. latest
200. tenir	verb	run; hold
201. cet	pronoun (demonstrative)	this; that
202. main	noun	hand
203. cela	pronoun (demonstrative; formal contexts)	this; that
204. vite	1. adverb 2. adjective	1. quickly; soon 2. fast
205. oublier	verb	forget

206. air	noun	look; appearance
207. salut	noun	greeting
208. fils	noun	son
209. travailler	verb	work; practice
210. moins	adverb	less
211. tête	noun	face; head
212. coup	noun	punch; kick; blow
213. écouter	verb	listen
214. raison	noun	reason
215. manger	verb	eat
216. amour	noun	love
217. entrer	verb	enter; come in
218. dont	pronoun (interrogative)	whose

219. nouveau	adjective	new
220. devenir	verb	become
221. hein	expression	What?; Eh?
222. commencer	verb	start; begin
223. merde	expression/interjection	Crap!
224. moment	noun	moment
225. voiture	noun	car
226. vieux	1. adjective 2. noun	1. old 2. old woman; old man
227. demain	noun	tomorrow
228. revoir	noun	goodbye
229. elles	pronoun (plural feminine)	they
230. payer	verb	pay

231. fou	1. adjective 2. noun	1. crazy 2. fool; madman
232. tirer	verb	pull
233. ouvrir	verb	open
234. oeil	noun	eye; view
235. fait	noun	fact; event
236. changer	verb	change; exchange
237. question	noun	question; matter
238. tomber	verb	fall
239. assez	adverb	fairly; enough
240. foutre	verb	to do; give
241. excuser	verb	excuse; forgive
242. affaire	noun	business;

		affair
243. dormir	verb	sleep
244. combien	adverb	how many; how much
245. frère	noun	brother
246. travail	noun	work; employment
247. idée	noun	idea
248. eh	expression/interjection	Hey!
249. puis	1. adjective 2. adverb 3. preposition	1. next 2. then; besides 3. plus
250. famille	noun	family
251. truc	noun	thing; trick
252. trois	noun	three

253. tant	adverb	much
254. souvenir	1. verb 2. noun	1. remember 2. souvenir; memory
255. ni	conjunction	nor; or
256. tous	pronoun	all; everything
257. occuper	verb	occupy
258. entre	preposition	among; between
259. ok	expression	OK!
260. marcher	verb	march; walk
261. chance	noun	chance; luck
262. aujourd'hui	1. noun 2. adverb	1. today 2. nowadays
263. envoyer	verb	send; throw; dispatch

264. histoire	noun	history; story
265. jeune	1. adjective 2. noun	1. young; youthful 2. young person
266. tard	1. adverb 2. tardy	1. late 2. tardy
267. apprendre	verb	learn; hear about
268. minute	noun	minute
269. boire	verb	drink (alcohol)
270. garder	verb	guard; look after
271. quelques	adjective	some; a few
272. type	noun	type; kind
273. porte	noun	door; gate

274. montrer	verb	show
275. attention	noun	attention
276. asseoir	verb	sit; sit down; sit up
277. porter	verb	carry; wear
278. mec	noun	guy; man
279. année	noun	year
280. sous	preposition	under
281. prêt	adjective	ready
282. contre	preposition	against
283. prier	verb	pray
284. pendant	preposition	during
285. mois	noun	month
286. meilleur	adjective	best; better
287. servir	verb	serve
288. madame	noun	Mrs.; madam

289. putain	slang (vulgar)	hooker; tramp
290. écrire	verb	write
291. part	noun	part; portion; share
292. eau	noun	water
293. sang	noun	blood
294. place	noun	room
295. espérer	verb	hope
296. plein	adjective	full; solid
297. désoler	verb	upset
298. eux	pronoun	them; they
299. retrouver	verb	find; meet
300. ville	noun	city; town

Congratulations! You've made it to the end of one of the most essential language lessons for beginners. Give yourself a pat on the back, because now you have a full 65% comprehension of the French language. You're on the fastest route to fluency. From here, all that's left to do is build your vocabulary and learn the proper syntax for creating French sentences.

Chapter 6: Noun Genders and Plurals

Nouns are used extensively in every language and dialect of the world—absolutely no exception. Since they form the basis of nearly every phrase and sentence imaginable, nouns are incredibly important in spoken and written language. Any language course would be incomplete without a lesson on nouns and how to properly build sentences around them. Fortunately, nouns are fairly basic, thus, they are the easiest language elements to learn.

Nouns play the same role in every language: they identify a person, place, object, or idea. Like English, every sentence in French depends on nouns to be complete. Without them, your French skills would be limited to senseless sentence fragments.

Determining Noun Gender

The first thing to remember about French nouns is that they are either feminine or masculine. A noun's gender has an influence on the article preceding it—e.g. *le* (masculine), *la* (feminine), *un* (masculine), or *une* (feminine)—pronouns, and the ending of adjectives and verbs. In most cases, a noun's suffix indicates its specific gender. However, there are many exceptions to gender pattern rules.

As you build your French vocabulary, it's important to determine the gender of each new noun you learn. Take a look at the gender rules in the table below. It will act as a reference guide for determining the specific gender of the French nouns listed in this chapter, as well as nouns you learn beyond the pages of this book.

Masculine	Feminine
Nouns that refer to male people.	Nouns that refer to female people.
Nouns that refer to animals of the male species, e.g. *étalon* (stallion), *cerf* (stag).	Nouns that refer to animals of the female species, e.g. *louve* (female wolf), *chatte* (female cat).
Names of cities, towns, countries, nature terms, and other places—excluding those ending in -e.	Most place names that end in -e.

Nouns with the following suffixes:	Nouns with the following suffixes:
-age	-ée
-il, -ail, -eil, -ueil	-tè
-ment	-ière
-er	-ie
-é, with the exception of *té*	-ure
-eau	-ude
-ou	-ade
-ème, -ège	-ance,
-i, -at, -et, -ot	-ence
-oir	-ine
-isme	-ise
-ing	-alle
-ard	-elle
-most nouns ending with	-esse

consonants	-ette

For a more comprehensive gender pattern table, refer to frenchtogether.com/french-nouns-gender. If you're not sure on the gender of a specific French noun, feel free to look it up. After all, Google is a harmless, helpful tool!

French Plurals

In terms of plurals, French and English are very much alike. In most cases, plural nouns are formed by simply adding -s to the end of a singular French noun. There are, however, a few exceptions to keep in mind:

- French words ending in the letter S can be either singular or plural. In other words, there is no need to add a -s to the end of these words—they are already plural.

- The spelling of words ending in -x and -z does not change between their singular and plural forms, just like words ending in -s.

- Singular words ending in -al, -ail, and -au are turned to plural by changing their suffix to -aux, e.g. *général* (singular) becomes *généraux* (plural).

- Singular words ending in -ou and -eu become plural by adding -x to their ending, e.g. *bijou* (singular) becomes *bijoux* (plural).

The final -s in plural nouns is not usually pronounced.

Plural Articles

As previously mentioned, nouns directly influence the article preceding them, depending on whether they are singular or plural. Singular French nouns are preceded by singular articles and pronouns, e.g. *un* and *la*. Plural nouns, however, are preceded by plural articles and pronouns.

The table below shows the plural forms of French articles and pronouns:

Singular Article	Plural Form
la	les
le	les
l'	les
un	des

une	des
du	des
de la	des
de l’	des
je	nous
tu	vous
il	Ils
elle	elles

Now that you’re aware of the general rules associated with masculine and feminine nouns, as well as singular and plural forms of nouns, it’s time to build your vocabulary. Whenever you learn a new French noun, identify whether the word is feminine or masculine, and make a note of the gender. Oftentimes, you will be able to determine the gender of a noun by just simply reading it; other times, you’ll have to search it. The more you practice the French language, the easier it will be to determine noun genders. Likewise, the easier it will be to designate the proper article to a plural noun.

Chapter 7: French Numerals, Date, and Time

Numbers are one of those things you just can't get away from. They're commonly brought up in daily conversation no matter the language. As inescapable little nouns, you need numbers to specify the date, tell time, or to simply ask for a dozen eggs at a market. Numbers are to language-learning as sunlight is to plants. For this reason, numbers will be the first nouns you learn in your French-speaking endeavors.

The good news with numbers is that they're always constant—unlike other objects that change in word form, from singular to plural, to past and present tense. Even better, you only need to be able to count to 30 in French to master all French numbers. Thankfully, numbers are relatively easily to memorize regardless of the complexity of a particular language. Their order follows a specific pattern that you may notice from the table below. Chances are you'll breeze right through this lesson.

Repetition is the name of the game in this chapter. If you're feeling up to it, try saying the numbers up to 30 aloud in a singsong "ABC" manner; you'll memorize them more efficiently by associating them with a common melody.

Number	French
0	zéro
1	un
2	deux
3	trois
4	quatre
5	cinq
6	six
7	sept
8	huit
9	neuf
10	dix
11	onze
12	douze
13	treize

14	quatorze
15	quinze
16	seize
17	dix-sept
18	dix-huit
19	dix-neuf
20	vingt
21	vingt et un
22	vingt-deux
23	vingt-trois
24	vingt-quatre
25	vingt-cinq
26	vingt-six
27	vingt-sept
28	vingt-huit
29	vingt-neuf

30	trente
40	quarente
50	cinquante
60	soixante
70	soixante-dix
80	quatre-vingts
90	quatre-vingt-dix
100	cent
1,000	mille
10,000	dix mille
1,000,000	un million

From 30, you would continue with*trente et un* (31), *trente-deux* (32), *trente-trois* (33), and so on, and so forth. It's fairly self-explanatory as numerical order follows a specific numerical pattern.

Notice, however, that 70 is basically 60+10, 80 is counted as four twenties, and 90 is counted as four twenties plus ten. From this pattern, you would continue counting from 70 by saying the number word for 60+11 (71), 60+12 (72), and so on. Luckily, French fluency doesn't depend on full knowledge of numbers. As mentioned earlier in the chapter, 30 is the ideal level for the highest French numerical knowledge. In fact, you now have a good enough knowledge of numbers to move on to dates!

The French Calendar

Learning the fundamentals of the French calendar enables you to properly talk dates in French. This portion of the lesson is extremely easy to master, because just like French numbers, days and months remain constant—no tenses, no plurals.

Days of the Week

The term "days of the week" is translated to French as *les jours de la semaine*. The days of the week are always masculine. The French week starts on Monday, as opposed to Sunday in the American week. Also, days aren't capitalized in French.

Day	**French**
Monday	lundi

Tuesday	mardi
Wednesday	mercredi
Thursday	jeudi
Friday	vendredi
Saturday	samedi
Sunday	dimanche

Months of the Year

Yet another easy group of nouns to remember is the months of the year—or as you would say in French, *les mois de l'année*. Like the days of the week, French months are masculine nouns. They aren't capitalized either.

Month	**French**
January	janvier
February	février
March	mars
April	avril

May	mai
June	juin
July	juillet
August	août
September	septembre
October	octobre
November	novembre
December	décembre

Notice that French months begin with the same letter as English months. They're cognates as well, thus making memorization a piece of cake.

When you're writing French dates, follow the format "day month year." Commas are unnecessary in terms of written dates. So, August 23, 2015 would be written as "23 août 2015."

Verbalizing dates is just as simple. If you've memorized the French numbers from 1 to 30 by now, saying dates aloud should be an easy task. Simply add the French article *le* to the beginning, and read all dates as cardinal numbers.

Let's say the date is March 15, 2015. In French, you would say *"le quinze mars deux mille quatorze."* If a native French speaker were to ask you what day it is, and it's Wednesday, June 5th, you would reply with, *"mercredi cinq juin."*

Here are some sample sentences regarding the date and day of the week:

Q: **Quelle est la date aujourd'hui?** (What is the date today?)
A: *Aujourd'hui c'est le lundi 10 septembre.* (Today is Monday, September 10th.

Q: **Quel jour sommes-nous aujourd'hui?** (What is the date today?)
A: *Aujourd'hui c'est mardi.* (Today is Tuesday.)

Telling Time in French

If you know how to read a clock and you have a thorough knowledge of French cardinal numbers, then you already know how to tell time in French. It's as simple as saying the numbers.

Here are a few examples:

Time	French
1:30	une-heure trente
2:00	deux-heures
2:15	deux-heures quinze
3:50	trois-heures cinquante
4:26	quatre-heures vingt-six
5:32	cinq-heures trente-deux
6:45	six-heures quarante-cinq
8:05	huit-heures zéro cinq
12:25	douze-heures vingt-cinq

They say if it was easy, you probably didn't do it right. Not in the case of telling time in French; it really is an easy system. Notice that the hour of one o'clock is not plural, hence the singular article *un* and the singular form of the word "hour" (*heure*) is used. The rest is written in plural French form.

You might be wondering why the time of day, i.e. A.M. and P.M. isn't clarified in the times shown in the table above. There is no equivalent of A.M. and P.M in telling time in French. There are, however, four simple time-words that you can link to the end of French times in order to specify the time of day. The following expressions are extremely important to remember when telling time in French:

- *du matin* (in the morning)

- *de l'après-midi* (in the afternoon)

- *du soir* (in the evening)

- *de la nuit* (in the night)

For example, to express 1:00PM in French, you would say *"une-heure de l'après-midi."* 7:45 in the morning would be translated to *"sept-heures quarante-cinq du matin."* It's as simple as that!

To ask someone what time it is in French, simply say *"Quelle heure est-t-il?"* A reply to such a question should follow the format *"Il est* + the number + *heure* + time of day."

Chapter 8: Common French Nouns

Adding more and more nouns to your French vocabulary is a fundamental step in your language-learning strategy. While numbers form the most basic nouns in all languages, they don't carry much value when it comes to actual daily interactions.

You're already well aware of the importance of nouns to proper sentence function. It's nearly impossible to form a phrase—much less a sentence—without a definite subject—in other words, nouns. So before you begin your phrase-building exercises, it's important to first fill your French vocabulary with common nouns brought up in every day conversation. The tables in this chapter categorize some of the most frequently used nouns in the French language.

Parts of the Body

When you're a beginner in a new language, it's important to start small and work your way up to more complex sentence structures. After all, you have to learn to walk before you can run. So no matter how basic the topic of a particular language lesson, it shouldn't be written off as irrelevant. You'd be surprised at how often basic words are brought up in ordinary conversation.

As you practice memorizing the parts of the body, write down their gender and plural form. Feel free to check your answers with a translator tool online.

Part of the Body	French Translation
head	tête
face	visage
nose	nez
mouth	bouche
eye	oeil
cheeks	joues
eae	oreille
chin	menton
hair	cheveux
lip	lèvre
heart	coeur
neck	cou

teeth	dents
throat	gorge
tongue	langue
tooth	dent
stomach	estomac
finger	doigt
hand	main
arm	bras
foot	pied
toe	orteil
leg	jambe
knee	genou
thigh	cuisse
chest	poitrine
elbow	coude
shoulder	épaule

back	dos

Animals

While animals aren't necessarily considered a common topic in daily French conversation, they're a great theme to study. You'll need a lot of French nouns later when you begin building phrases out of nouns, adjectives, and verbs. To help you out, I've added the proper "the" article before each animal below based on gender.

Animal	French Translation
chicken	le poulet
cow	la vache
pig	le cochon
sheep	le mouton
donkey	l'âne
llama	le lama
duck	le canard
horse	le cheval

mule	la mule
goat	la chèvre
mouse	la souris
goose	l'oie
butterfly	le papillon
bee	l'abeille
spider	l'araignée
ant	la fourmi
snail	l'escargot
dog	le chien
cat	le chat
parrot	le perroquet
hamster	le hamster
gerbil	la gerbille
ferret	le furet
goldfish	le poisson rouge

bear	l'ours
antelope	l’antilope
bat	le chauve-souris
bird	l'oiseau
elk	l'élan
deer	le cerf
beaver	le castor
fox	le renard
owl	le hibou
otter	la loutre
moose	l'orignal
raccoon	le raton-laveur
rabbit	le lapin
porcupine	le porc-épic
wolf	le loup
squirrel	l'écureil

elephant	l'éléphant
hippopotamus	l'hippopotame
giraffe	la girafe
zebra	le zèbre
ape	le singe
baboon	le babouin
camel	le chameau
buffalo	le buffle
cheetah	le guépard
coyote	le coyote
gorilla	la gorille
gazelle	la gazelle
kangaroo	le kangourou
jaguar	le jaguar
leopard	le léopard
lion	le lion

monkey	le singe
panda	le panda
panther	le panthère
ostrich	l'autruche
rhinoceros	le rhinocéros
tiger	le tigre
turtle	la tortue
toad	le crapaud
frog	la grenouille
alligator	l'alligator
crocodile	le crocodile
snake	le serpent
lizard	le lézard
crab	le crabe
dolphin	le dauphin
eel	l'anguille

jellyfish	la méduse
lobster	le homard
manatee	le lamantin
pelican	le pélican
penguin	le pingouin
sea lion	l'otarie
walrus	le morse
whale	la baleine
shark	le requin

People

Continue building your noun vocabulary with words regarding the many professions in the world. Try to figure out the proper "a/an" (*un/*une) French article that should precede each noun below. It would help to attach a mental picture to the word you are memorizing.

Profession	**French Translation**

actor	acteur
actress	actrisse
farmer	agriculteur
architect	architecte
astronaut	astronaute
lawyer	avocat
pastor	berger
jeweller	bijoutier
butcher	boucher
baker	boulanger
singer	chanteur
taxi driver	chauffeur de taxi
surgeon	chirurgien
hairdresser	coiffeur
accountant	comptable
caretaker	concierge

driver	conducteur
consultant	conseiller
foreman	contremaître
shoemaker	cordonnier
cook	cuisinier
priest	curé
dentist	dentiste
servant	domestique
writer	écrivain
electrician	électricien
employee	employé
nurse	enfermière
student	étudiant
postman	facteur
engineer	ingénieur
gardener	jardinier

journalist	journaliste
judge	juge
builder	maçon
model	mannequin
sailor	marin
mechanic	mécanicien
doctor	médecin
miner	mineur
monk	moine
instructor	moniteur
nanny	nounou
laborer	ouvrier
fisherman	pêcheur
painter	peintre
chemist	pharmacien
pilot	pilote

plumber	plombier
policeman	policier
politician	politicien
fireman	pompier
teacher	professeur
psychiatrist	psychiatre
receptionist	réceptionniste
nun	religieuse
reporter	reporter
scientist	scientifique
secretary	secrétaire
waiter	serveur
soldier	soldat
tailor	tailleur d'habit
technician	technicien
bullfighter	toreador

salesman	vendeur
veterinarian	vétérinaire

Places

Place	French Translation
town hall	hótel de ville
library	bibliothèque
museum	musée
court	tribunal
post office	bureau de poste
police station	poste de police
prison	prison
barracks	caserne
fire station	caserne de pompiers
hospital	hôpital
school	école

university	université
church	église
castle	château
cathedral	cathédrale
art gallery	galerie d'art
cinema	cinéma
theater	théâtre
bank	banque
cemetery	cimetière
airport	aéroport
market	marché
train station	gare
stadium	stade
park	parc
mall	centre commercial
house	maison

barbershop	salon de coiffure
store	magasin
deli	épicerie fine
supermarket	supermarche
restaurant	restaurant

Everyday Objects

The final nouns you will learn in this book are listed below—a collection of everyday objects. It's a good idea to remember them as you will rely heavily on them in later chapters—particularly in your phrase-building exercises. *AnkiDroid Flashcards* is a great app for building your own flashcards deck, which you can carry around in a convenient digital format.

Object	**English Translation**
airplane	avion
airport	aéroport
angel	ange
apple	pomme

aunt	tante
backpack	sac à dos
baggage	bagages
balloon	ballon
banana	banane
bathroom	salle de bain
bathtub	baignoire
bed	lit/plumard
belt	ceinture
bench	banc
bible	bible
blanket	couverture
boat	bateau
book	livre
bowl	bol
boyfriend	petit-ami

bread	pain
breakfast	petit déjeuner
broom	balai
brother	frère
bush	buisson
butter	beurre
cabinet	placard
cake	gâteau
calculator	calculatrice
can	boîte
candy	bonbon
car	voiture
carpet	moquette
cash register	caisse
cell phone	portable/mobile
chair	chaise

check	chèque
cheese	fromage
chocolate	chocolat
closet	penderie
clothes	vétements
cloud	nuage
coat	manteau
coffee	café
computer	ordinateur
couch	canapé
cup	tasse
dad	papa
daughter	fille
dawn	aube
desk	bureau
dessert	dessert

dictionary	dictionnaire
dining room	salle à manger
dinner	dîner
door	porte
drawing	dessin
dress	robe
dresser	commode
earrings	boucles d’oreilles
egg	oeuf
English	anglais
fall/autumn	automne
family	famille
father	père
fireplace	cheminée
fish	poisson
flower	fleur

fog	brouillard
folder	chemise
food	nourriture
fork	fourchette
France	France
French	français
french fries	frites
friend	ami
fruit	fruit
furniture	meuble
garbage	ordures
garden	jardin
gate	porte
girlfriend	petit-amie
gloves	gants
glue	colle

grandfather	grand-père
grandmother	grand-mère
grass	pelouse
guitar	guitare
hanger	cintre
hat	chapeau
herb	herbe
honey	miel
husband	mari
ice	glace
jacket	veste
juice	jus
ketchup	ketchup
kitchen	cuisine
knife	couteau
lake	lac

lamp	lampee
lemon	citron
light	lumière
living room	salle de séjour
lunch	déjeuner
menu	menu
microwave	four à micro-ondes
milk	lait
mirror	miroir
mom	maman
money	argent
moon	lune
mop	balai à franges
morning	midi
mother	mère
motorcycle	motorcyclette

mountain	montagne
movie	film
music	musique
mustard	moutarde
napkin	serviette
nephew	neveu
newspaper	journal
niece	nièce
nightstand	table de nuit
notebook	carnet
novel	roman
ocean	ocèan
oven	four
painting	peinture
pants	pantalon
paper	papier

pen	stylo
pencil	crayon
pepper	poivre
piano	piano
pillow	oreiller
pitcher	cruche
plant	plante
plate	assiette
pond	étang
purse	sac à main
radio	radio
rag	chiffon
rain	pluie
receipt	reçu
refrigerator	réfrigérateur
restroom	toilette

Ring	bague
River	fleuve
Room	piéce
Salad	salade
Salt	sel
Sand	sable
sandals	sandales
Sea	mer
Shelf	étagère
Shirt	chemise
shoes	chaussures
shorts	short
Sink	lavabo
sister	soeur
Skirt	jupe
Sky	ciel

soap	savon
socks	chaussette
sofa	sofa
soil	sol
son	fils
soup	potage/soupe
sponge	éponge
spoon	cuillère
spring	printemps
stairs	escalier
stapler	agrafeuse
story	histoire
stove	cuisiniére
subway	métro
sugar	sucre
suit	costume

suitcase	valise
summer	été
Sun	soleil
sunglasses	lunettes de soleil
sweater	pull
Table	table
Taxi	taxi
Tea	thé
television	télévision
Test	essai
ticket	billet
Tie	cravate
toilet	toilette
towel	serviette
Train	train
Tree	arbre

truck	camion
uncle	oncle
United States	Etats-Unis
vacuum	aspirateur
vase	vase
water	eau
wife	femme
window	fenêtre
wine	vin
winter	huver
zipper	fermeture

Adjectives are another part of speech that play an important role in sentence structure. They're found in every language of the world, and you'll be using adjectives in French all the time. You may remember from English class that an adjective is a word which describes a noun. Whether the noun is a person, place, tangible object, or an abstract idea, any word that modifies it is an adjective.

This chapter marks the beginning of learning French phrases. Build your own simple two-word phrases by pairing a noun with an adjective from the table below. Your phrases should follow the format adjective + noun, e.g. *bleu ballon* (blue balloon). With so many nouns and adjectives to choose from, the possibilities are endless.

All the adjectives listed in the table are masculine; they can be made feminine by changing their suffix to a feminine one. To do this, keep the following rules in mind:

- Feminine singular adjectives are formed by simply adding -e to the end of the basic masculine form.

- If an adjective already ends in -e in its masculine singular form, there is no change.

- If an adjective ends in -on or -ien in its masculine singular form, the feminine singular form is formed by doubling the final consonant and adding a second -e. For example, the masculine singular adjective *bon* would be *bonne* in its feminine form.

- A similar rule applies to adjectives ending in -el, -ul, and -eil. To turn such adjectives into their feminine singular form, simply double the final consonant and add -e to the very end, e.g. *nul* becomes *nulle*.

- If an adjective ends in -et in its masculine singular form, the feminine singular is formed by substituting the suffix -et with -ette, e.g. *net* becomes *nette*.

- If an adjective ends in -ot in its masculine singular form, the feminine singular is formed by adding an -e to the end, e.g. *idiot* becomes *idiote*.

- If an adjective ends in -er in its masculine singular form, the feminine singular is formed by substituting the suffix -er with -ère, e.g. *cher* becomes *chère, léger* becomes *légère*.

- If an adjective ends in -f in its masculine singular form, the feminine singular is formed by simply changing the -f to a -ve, e.g. *naïf* becomes *naïve*.

- If an adjective ends in -x in its masculine singular form, the feminine singular is formed by eliminating the -x and adding -se to the end, e.g. *nerveux* becomes *nerveuse*.

- If an adjective ends in -s in its masculine singular form, the feminine singular is formed by adding -e to the end, e.g. *gris* becomes *grise*.

- Finally, if an adjective ends in -c in its masculine singular form, the feminine singular is formed by substituting the suffix -c with -che, e.g. *blanc* becomes *blanche*.

Adjective	**French Translation**

alike	pareil
alive	vivant
alone	seul
ancient	ancien
angry	fâché
annoyed	ennuyé
athletic	sportif
bad	mauvise
beautiful	beau
beloved	cher
better	meilleur
big	grand
bitter	amer
black	noir
blue	bleu
boring	ennuyeux

brave	courageux
bright	clair
brown	brun
cheap	bon marché
clean	propre
cloudy	nuageux
cold	froid
complete	entier
confident	assuré
confused	désorienté
cool	frais
cowardly	lâche
crooked	tordue
cunning	malin
dark	foncé
deep	profond

definite	certain
delighted	ravi
different	autre
difficult	difficile
dirty	noir
dry	sec
early	premier
easy	facile
elderly	âgé
embarrassed	confus
empty	vide
energetic	énergique
exhausted	épuisé
expensive	cher
fair	juste
fake	faux

far	éloigné
fat	gros
filthy	sale
foggy	du brouillard
foreign	étranger
free	libre
freezing	gèle
fresh	frais
friendly	amical
full	plein
funny	drôle
glad	heureux
gold	doré
good	bon
gray	gris
green	vert

happy	content
hard	dur
hardworking	travailleur
healthy	en bonne santé
heavy	lourd
honest	droit
hot	chaud
humble	pauvre
humid	humide
impatient	impatient
interesting	intéressant
kind	gentip
last	dernier
lazy	paresseux
lifeless	mort
light	léger

lonely	solitaire
loud	bruyant
mean	méchant
naive	naïf
narrow	étroit
natural	naturel
near	proche
nervous	nerveux
new	nouveau
next	prochain
nice	sympa
odd	bizzare
old	vieux
open-minded	sans préjugés
orange	orange
ordinary	ordinaire

outgoing	ouvert
patient	patient
patriotic	patriotique
pink	rose
playful	taquin
powerful	puissant
pretty	joli
purple	violet
quiet	silencieus
ready	prêt
red	rouge
rough	rugeux
sad	triste
salty	salé
same	même
scared	effrayé

Serious	sérieux
Short	court
Shy	timide
Sick	malade
Silver	argenté
Slow	lent
Small	petit
Smart	intelligent
Smooth	lisse
snobbish	snob
Soft	mol
Solemn	grave
sophisticated	raffiné
Sorry	navré
Sour	aigre
Spicy	épicé

stormy	orageux
straight	droit
strange	étrange
strong	fort
stupid	stupide
sunny	du soleil
sweet	doux
tall	haut
Tan	bronzé
thick	gros
thin	mince
tired	fatigué
true	vrai
ugly	laid
unfriendly	froid
unhappy	malhereux

Warm	chaud
Weak	faible
Wet	humide
White	blanc
Windy	du vent
Worried	inquiet
Wrong	faux
Yellow	jaune
Young	jeune

Chapter 10: Past and Present French Verbs

Verbs are words that convey action. As the action word in a sentence, a verb tells you what is happening, what has happened, what is going to happen, name an action, indicate a state of being, or describe a feeling. When paired with an article and a noun, it forms basic phrases and short sentences such as *Le chien court* (The dog runs.)

In English, there are three distinct tenses for verbs: present, past, and future. Since you are still in the beginner levels of French, we will only focus on verbs in the present tense. In English present tense, there are only two verb forms, e.g. sing and sings. French verbs, on the other hand, have up to six verb forms. These conjugations are different for each grammatical person.

Take the French word *chanter*, meaning "sing" in the present tense. You have the following possibilities:

- *je chante*
- *tu chantes*
- *il chante*

- *nous chantons*
- *vous chantez*
- *ils chantent*

Having six different conjugations for each verb just in the present tense brings about a lot of confusion. However, you don't need an extensive knowledge of French verbs to attain fluency. Focus first on memorizing the common verbs used in present tense in the French language. Once you're accustomed to present tense verbs, you will be ready to move on to other tenses. I've included the past tense of each verb below to strengthen your vocabulary further.

Verb	French Present Tense	French Past Tense
Accept	accepter	accepté
Allow	permettre	permis
Begin	commencer	commencé
believe	croire	considéré

borrow	emprunter	emprunté
break	casser	cassé
bring	apporter	apporté
buy	acheter	acheté
cancel	annuler	annulé
change	changer	changé
clean	laver	lavé
comb	peigner	peigné
complain	se plaindre	plaints
cook	cuisinier	cuit
cough	tousser	toussé
count	compter	compté
cry	pleurer	pleuré
cut	couper	coupé
dance	danser	dansé
draw	dessiner	dessiné

Drive	conduire	conduite
Eat	manger	mangé
explain	expliquer	expliqué
Fall	tomber	tombé
Fill	remplir	rempli
Find	trouver	trouvé
Finish	terminer	terminé
Fix	fixer	fixé
Give	donner	donné
Go	aller	allé
Hear	entendre	entendu
Hold	tenir	tenue
Know	savoir	savait
Learn	apprendre	appris
Listen	écouter	ecouté
Live	vivre	vivait

look	regarder	regardé
lose	perdre	perdu
make	faire	fabriqué
mix	mélanger	mélangé
move	déménager	déménagé
open	ouvrir	ouvert
organize	organiser	organisé
pay	payer	payé
play	jouer	joué
rain	pleuvoir	plu
reply	répondre	répondu
say	dire	dit
see	voir	vu
sell	vendre	vendu
send	envoyer	envoyé
shove	pousser	poussé

Sign	signer	signé
Sing	chanter	chanté
Sit	s'asseoir	sam
Sleep	dormir	dormi
Smile	sourire	sourit
Smoke	fumer	fumé
Spend	dépenser	dépensé
Study	étudier	étudiè
Swim	nager	nagé
Take	prendre	pris
Talk	parler	parlé
Teach	enseigner	enseigné
Tell	dire	raconté
Think	penser	pensée
translate	traduire	traduit
Travel	voyager	voyagé

try	essayer	essaye
understand	comprendre	entendu
use	utiliser	utilisé
wait	attendre	attendu
watch	regarder	regardé
work	travailler	travaillé
write	écrire	écrite

As you can see, verb tense follows a pattern. In cases where French present tense verbs end in -er, their past tense can be found by simply substituting the suffix for -é. Now that you have a suitable knowledge of French verbs, try building article + noun + verb phrases. Pay close attention to detail and run your phrases through an online translator to check for mistakes.

Chapter 11: Useful French Expressions

Now that you've got the basics of French down, and you have the capability of building simple phrases, you're well on your way toward fluency. I leave you with a collection of useful French expressions.

English	French
Welcome.	Bienvenue.
Hello.	Bonjour.
How are you?	Comment allez-vous?
I am fine, thank you. And you?	Ça va bien, merci. Et toi?
What's your name?	Comment t'appelles-tu
Long time no see.	Ça fait longtemps.
What's new?	Quoi de neuf?
Where are you from?	D'où viens-tu?

How old are you?	Quel âge as-tu?
Pleased to meet you.	Enchanté.
Good morning.	Bonjour.
Good afternoon.	Bon après-midi.
Good evening.	Bonsoir.
Good night.	Bonne nuit.
Goodbye!	Au revoir.
Good luck!	Bonne chance!
Cheers!	Santé!
Enjoy your meal.	Bon appétit.
Have a nice day.	Bonne journée.
Have a good journey.	Bon voyage.
I understand.	Je comprends.
I don't understand.	Je ne comprends pas.
Yes.	Oui.
No.	Non.

Maybe.	Peut-être.
I don’t know.	Je ne sais pas.
Do you speak English?	Parlez vous anglais?
Excuse me.	Excusez-moi.
How much is this?	C’est combien?
Sorry.	Désolé.
Please.	S’il vous plaît.
Really?	Sérieux?
Thank you.	Merci.
Thank you very much.	Merci beaucoup.
No problem!	Ça n’est pas grave!
You’re welcome.	De rien.
I love you.	Je t’aime
I miss you.	Tu me manques.
I agree with you.	He suis d’accord.
Stop!	Arrêtez!

What's this?	Qu'est-ce que c'est?
Is that right/wrong?	Est-ce correct/incorrect?
Can you help me?	Peux-tu m'aider?
Can I help you?	Puis-je t'aider?
I'll be right back.	Je reviens tout de suite.
Happy birthday!	Joyeux anniversaire!
Happy New Year!	Bonne année!
Merry Christmas!	Joyeux Noël!
Congratulations!	Félicitations!
Bless you.	A vos souhaits.
Sweet dreams.	Fais de beaux rêves.
I'm hungry.	J'ai faim.
It was nice meeting you!	Je suis ravi de t'avoir rencontré!
It was nice talking to you!	J'ai été ravi de te parler!
You look beautiful!	Tu es ravissante!

One moment please.	Un moment s'il-vous-plaît.
Are you sure?	Es-tu certain?

****** PREVIEW OTHER BOOKS BY THIS AUTHOR******

Excerpt from the first 3 Chapters

"ONE WEEK POTUGUESE MASTERY" by Erica Stewart

Chapter 1: Introduction

Differences between English and Portuguese

Portuguese is a Romance language and part of the Indo-European language family. It is closely related to Spanish. The Portuguese spoken in Europe and the Portuguese spoken in Brazil are further apart in terms of pronunciation, spelling and vocabulary than the English spoken in England and the English spoken in the USA.

We can divide the difference between these languages in some categories, and they are: alphabet, phonology, grammar and vocabulary.

Alphabet

The Portuguese alphabet consists of 23 letters (lacking the K, W and Y of the English alphabet), plus 11 letters with diacritics such as the Ç. Punctuation corresponds largely to that in English. The English writing system, therefore, presents little difficulty to Portuguese learners.

Phonology

Brazilian Portuguese is a syllable-timed language, in contrast to English. This can result in learners having serious difficulty reproducing the appropriate intonation patterns of spoken English. This is less of a problem for European Portuguese speakers, whose Portuguese variety is stress-timed like English. Portuguese contains about 9 vowel sounds and 19 consonant sounds. This is fewer than English, and there are fewer consonant clusters.

Grammar

Much of the English verb system will be familiar to Portuguese learners since the same features exist in their own language. However, some significant differences exist, which may lead to mistakes of negative transfer. Portuguese word order is a little more flexible than that of English; and there are variations between the two languages in the placement of adjectives, adverbials or pronouns and in the syntax of sentences containing indirect speech. However, basic Portuguese sentence structure is similar to that of English so learners have no especial difficulty expressing their ideas comprehensibly.

Vocabulary

Because of shared Latin roots there are many English/Portuguese cognates, which can facilitate the acquisition of a strong academic vocabulary.

Learning the Pronunciation

Pronunciation is arguably the most important aspect of learning a language. Of course, you don't have to be able to pronounce everything perfectly to be understood, and it will take time to get used to the strange sounds that you have to produce.

A few of the sounds in Portuguese can be difficult to imitate at first, because the sounds aren't used in English. But most people can understand what you're saying, even if you don't say every word perfectly. Many people think a foreign accent is charming, so don't worry about it.

There are a few things we must consider to get the

Portuguese pronunciation right! Let's start with the easy rules first.

1. Usually in Portuguese, words are stressed in the second last syllable.
2. Words ending with L, Z, R, U and I, are stressed in the LAST syllable.
3. Written accents are stronger than any other rule.
4. You normally read every single letter in a word, except the H that is always silent.

Portuguese alphabet

Let's start with something really basic, the alphabet

Aa Bb Cc Dd Ee Ff Gg Hh Ii Jj Kk Ll

Á bê Cê Dê é efe gê agá I jota capa ele

Mm Nn Oo Pp Qq Rr Ss Tt Uu Vv Ww

Emeene ó pê quê erreessetê u vê duplo-vê

Xx Yy Zz

Xis ípsilon zê

Portuguese diacritical marks

The tilde [~] – Used to denote a nasal sound

The acute accent [´] – Stress is placed on this syllable, and the vowel sound is open.

The grave accent [`] – Usually denotes 2 words squashed into one with the loss of a letter, but does not really affect pronunciation.

The circumflex accent [^] – Stress is placed on this syllable and the vowel sound is close.

Sounds of letters

Some letters in Portuguese have different sounds.

Let's start with the vowels:

A – like "a" in "ah"

Á - More open like in "cat"

À – Similar sound as "á" but only used alone, not in a word.

E – "Eh"

*Ê – "*Eh", but very short, almost silent (similar to French)

*É – "*Ay", as in "say"

I – “ee”, like in “Free”

O – “oo”

Ó - like ‘o’ in ‘hot’

Ô - like ‘oa’ in ‘coal’

U - like the last ‘u’ in ‘kung fu’.

And now let’s see the consonants:

C followed by “a,o,u” – K, a “c” that begins a word usually sound like a “k”

C followed by “e,i” – S

Ç – S, if the c has a hook-shaped mark under it, it makes an “s” sound

Ch – sh

G followed by “a,o,u” – hard “g” like in “go”

G followed by “e,i” – zh or J

Gu followed by “a” – gwa

Gu followed by “e,i” - hard “g” like in “go”

J - zh, like the s in "measure"

Lh - Like the "ll" in Spanish pronounciation. There is no English equivalent.

Nh - Just like the Spanish Ñ in "niño", or the French "gn" in "Champagne".

Qu followed by “a,ei” – Kw

Qu followed by “e,I” – K

Some examples

Let’s see some sentences. Try reading out loud.

These are normal sentences without diacritical marks.

The bold parts are the ones to be stressed:

- **Co**mo tem pa**ssa**do? (How has he been?)
- **Co**mo ele **co**me a co**mi**da. (How he eats food)
- O **li**vro tem **fo**lhas. (The book has leaves)
- As **fo**lhas do **li**vro **lem**bram **ou**tro **li**vro **ve**lho. (The book’s leaves remind of another old book)
- **E**les **com**pram **jor**nais e re**vis**tas. (They buy newspapers and magazines)

- A **mi**nha **pri**ma tem **ma**is **li**vros do que a **mi**nha vi**zi**nha. (My cousin has more books than my neighbour)

Now let's try examples with diacritical marks.

The diacritical marks are bolded:

- Hoje **é** quarta-feira. (Today is Wednesday)
- O gato subiu **à á**rvore e nunca mais desceu. (the cat ran up the tree, and hasn't come down since.)
- **Não são** permitidos elefantes no bar depois das oito horas. (Elephants are not permitted in the bar after eight o'clock.)
- Duas em cada tr**ê**s pessoas **não** entendem propor**ções** em mate**má**tica. (Three in two people do not understand proportions in mathematics.)
- O meu filho **é** um gangster frio e impla**cá**vel, e eu preciso de um abra**ç**o. (My son is a cold-hearted gangster, and I need a hug.)

Basic Grammar

Grammar is an essential part of any language, it's the

rules to which we obey and use to learn the language.

The good news is that grammar is not really that difficult. You just need to be realistic: it takes a few *years* to really get to grips with a language.

Nouns and Articles

Ok, here isn't where we are going to learn Portuguese vocabulary, we know that nouns it's the name we give to things. And before the nouns we have articles, and that's the important think we will learn.

To say "A", "An", or "Some" in Portuguese, you have 4 possibilities depending on gender and number. Gender, refers to words that are either feminine or masculine. Every single object, idea or person is either masculine or feminine - say male or female.

In English we have "The" as a definite article, but in Portuguese there isn't just one, so let's see how it works.

PT	EN
O (oo)	The masculine singular

Os (oosh) The masculine plural

A (ah) The feminine singular

As (ash) The feminine plural

A similar thing happens with the indefinite articles:

PT	EN	
Um (oong)	a or an	masculine singular
Uns (oongsh)	some	masculine plural
Uma (oomah)	a or an	feminine singular
Umas (oomash)	some	feminine plural

So let's see some examples to check if you really got this.

- livro - the book.
- As canetas - the pens.
- rato - the mouse.
- A filosofia - the philosophy.
- Os sonhos - The dreams.
- Um livro - a book.

- Uns livros - some books.
- Uma ideia - an idea.
- Umas ideias - some ideas.
- Uma caneta - a pen.
- Umas canetas - some pens.

Verbs

Verbs, something that gives us allot of work. There are so many different times of conjugation of verbs. But don't think it's hard and quit, we will do it look easy. It is after all an essential thing.

Here we will make it simple, we will teach the infinitive of some verbs and see the present conjugation.

Portuguese verbs are the words that give action to nouns, and that's the reason why they are very important.

Let's see the important question here: Who is doing the action?

PT	EN
Eu (Ehoo)	I or Me
Tu (too)	You
Ele (ay-lee)	He or Him

Ela (ay-lah) She or Her

Nós (nosh) We or Us

Vós (vosh) You (group)

Eles (ay-leesh) They or Them (male or mixed gender)

Elas (ay-lash) They or Them (female)

Adjectives

An adjective is a word whose main role is to modify a noun or pronoun, giving more information about the noun or pronoun's definition

Here are some rules to remember about adjectives in Portuguese:

- When talking about masculine things; end the adjective in an 'o'
- When talking about feminine things; end the adjective in an 'a'
- When talking about plural things that are masculine; end the adjective in 'os'
- When talking about plural things that are feminine; end the adjective in 'as'

- When talking about plural things that are both masculine and feminine end the adjective in ‘os’ because the masculine takes precedence over the feminine

Adverbs

Portuguese adverbs are part of speech. Generally they're words that modify any part of language other than a noun. Adverbs can modify verbs, adjectives (including numbers), clauses, sentences and other adverbs.

In Portuguese, adverbs are varied in their forms and context to express time, place, mode, quantity, intensity, affirmation, denial, doubt and exclusivity.

So let’s see some examples of each category.

ADVERBS THAT INDICATE TIME

PT EN

Hoje Today

Ontem Yesterday

Amanhã Tomorrow

Cedo Early

Tarde Late

Agora Now

Já Now

Adverbs that indicate place

PT	EN
Aqui	Here
Aí	There
Alí	Over there
Cá	Here
Lá	Over there

Adverbs that indicate denial

PT	EN
Não	No

Nunca	Never
Nem	Neither
Jamais	Never ever

Adverbs that indicate exclusivity

PT	EN
Só	Only
Somente	Just
Unicamente	Only
Apenas	Just
Senão	Otherwise

Prepositions

Prepositions are words which are used before a noun or pronoun to indicate their place, position, or time. Some verbs are also followed by prepositions.

The preposition must always agree with the word that follows it.

Most prepositions would begin with the link word ‘em’

and after the preposition would follow 'de'. These help put the preposition words into context and help the flow of sentences in Portuguese.

Prepositions of Location

The following prepositions are common in expressing location:

- ***à*** **- at**

A generally carries the meaning *to*. It means *at* in certain sentences.

Vamos nos ***sentar à mesa****?* - Let's sit at the table?

- **em**

Definite Article	Feminine		Masculine		Translation
	A	as	o	os	
Em +	*na*	*nas*	*no*	*nos*	on / in / at + the

Indefinite	Feminine		Masculine		Translation
	uma	umas	um	uns	

Articles					
Em +	*numa*	*numas*	*num*	*nuns*	on / in / at + a (or some(plural))

1. ***Em um*** *restaurante* - **In a** restaurant
2. *Estou* ***no*** *Brasil* - I am **in** Brazil
3. *O presente está* ***na*** *mesa.* - The gift is **on** the table.
4. *Ela mora* ***nos*** *Estados Unidos.* - She lives **in** the United States.

- ao longo [de] - along
- ao lado [de] - next [to]
- em redor [de] - around
- acima [de] / por cima [de] - above
- perto [de] - near
- debaixo [de] - under/below
- à frente [de] - in front of
- dentro [de] - in/inside
- atrás [de] - behind
- em cima [de] - on top [of]
- em frente [de] - in front [of]

- no meio [de] - in the center [of] / in the middle [of]
- entre - [in] between
- fora [de] - outside [of]

Prepositions of Direction

- a - to
- de - from
- através [de] - through
- sobre - over
- para - for/to

Other prepositions

- de - from [origin, possession, composition]
- para - for/in order to [recipient, goal]
- por - for/because of [cause]

	Feminine		Masculine		Translation
Definite Article	A	As	O	Os	
por+	pela	pelas	pelo	pelos	For / by / through + the

1. *Dou-te este presente pela tua ajuda.* - I give you this gift for you assistance.

2. *Estilhaços voaram pelas janelas.* - Shards flew through the windows.
3. *Enviei o cartão pelo correio.* - I sent the card by post.
4. *Luis caminhou pelos campos.* - Luis walked across the fields.

The use of the preposition "de"

Definite	Feminine		Masculine		Translation
Article	A	As	O	Os	
De+	da	das	do	dos	From / of + the

1. *O Brasil é o maior país da América Latina.* - Brazil is the largest country in Latin America.
2. *Ela não encontrou os agendas das amigas.* - She did not find her friends' notebooks.
3. *Ele gosta dos novos amigos.* - He likes the new friends.
4. *Eu sou do Perú.* - I am from Peru.

Excerpt from the first 3 Chapters

.